DOWN

Rebecca McCutcheon

Out-Spoken Press
London

Published by Out-Spoken Press,
PO Box 78744
London, N11 9FG

All rights reserved
© Rebecca McCutcheon

The rights of Rebecca McCutcheon to be identified as the author of this work have been asserted by them in accordance with section 77 of the Copyright, Designs and Patents Act 1988.

A CIP record for this title is available from the British Library.

This book is in copyright. Subject to statutory exception and to provisions of relevant collective licensing agreements, no reproduction of any part may take place without the written permission of Out-Spoken Press.

First edition published 2024
ISBN: 978-1-7384125-1-8

Typeset in Futura and Adobe Caslon
Design by Patricia Ferguson
Printed and bound by Print Resources

Out-Spoken Press is supported using public funding by the National Lottery through Arts Council England.

Supported using public funding by
ARTS COUNCIL ENGLAND

DOWN

CONTENTS

MUSIC FUTILITY	9
SOME HAVE GREATNESS	10
BEAR	11
RETCON	21
PAIN PERCEPTION OF CHICKEN EMBRYOS	23
THERE ARE NEURONS OF A NERVOUS SYSTEM	24
ODORIGUI	25
BIRTH	27
LET THE WORLD END	28
CAPACITY	29
BATTERY	30
CAMILLA	31
THE TIGER STAYED IN A TRAVELODGE	32
NATURE NURTURE	33
ANY CONSOLATION	34
PREDATOR THEORY	35
THE TIGER MAKES PROMISES	36
BEAR COUNTRY	37
IT'S TOO LATE FOR VISITORS	38
REASONABLE BELIEF	39
LATE ROOST	41
HANGOVER	42

STEPS TAKEN	43
LADY KLUCK	44
BLOOD IS THICKER	45
INDUSTRY	46
REMAINS	47
RITUALS	48
MIKE	49
IKIZUKURI	50
FAULTS	51
BILLINA	52
THE TIGER EVOLVES IMMUNITY	53
NIGHTLINES	54
RECOVERY LOOKS DIFFERENT ON EVERYONE	55
SALT & EGGS	57
PTEROTILLOMANIA	59
WITHOUT SLEEPING	60
LEAVE OF ABSENCE	61
ACKNOWLEDGEMENTS	63

for my Mum and Dad

MUSIC FUTILITY

the studio lights are black hot, three dead
wires coil on the floor starving for a piece
of god, I'm braced on the other side, a rug
fussy with age wonders if condensation
is the side effect of soundproofing a box
the canvas screens everything damp, you
taste of half a cigarette & instant coffee strong
like my adult teeth, I would rather be empty
mouthed for once but here I am glory-holed
drag me I won't mind how the carpet grips
are failing, they will trip the evening foxes
into the earth & anyway you have a son
who needs picking up

SOME HAVE GREATNESS

Great Yarmouth cracks its jaw; yawns at the dead season, where late roads
draw silent and black. Two bears stand guard in the sky, painted gold.

Great. They were news while they were taken down, and later rescued —
then the trail runs cold. This happened the year they were missing. Look up

what makes animals great and you'll find no answers; just white sharks
and plains rat snakes. As for places, territory has to be defined.

There are only eight species of bear alive today. None of them are great
just spectacled, sun or polar. You can double your life expectancy in captivity

but you'll have to decide if it's worth it. Nearly all bears are able to swim.
They don't all get the chance to prove they can get back out again.

A wind farm lies offshore. How much sea do you need to witness
for it to count, when almost half of all people who die by drowning

had no intention
                        of entering the water?

BEAR

The Guilt-Partridge hammers the crumbs left
on the table, asks what happened over breakfast

guesses when I don't answer. I'm being careless
with what I think about before sleeping. You convince

yourself you know impossible things; like *you can't die
in dreams* or *dogs don't perceive time*. The room grimaces.

A knot at the base of my spine keeps being pressed
flinching like the storm-touched trees in Yosemite.

I didn't know I could still feel lost in famous places.
Nothing's like the photos; trespassers on the rocks

flies in the woods. Mine don't show it either. I ignore
the speed limit, advice about storage, a still, red

bear on the granite. You know I'm never happy.
You try hard not to be, back away from every sign.

Every sign was right: bears attempt amazing feats
to take what you have in the dark. You don't have

to believe they deserve it. Each night you pull out
your metal box to lock it, hiding the scent of food

and your heart. You have nothing to spare. I find you
two ground squirrels wrestling, but no reasons why

I taste of berries, why wildfires sing for so long
in hot corners. They start thoughtlessly; three months

later they're still burning. There's a bear behind me.
I spread a damp palm in his fur, hungry and fearless.

A single piece of something human is all it takes
to tame an animal. I take him home, smiling

through customs, concealing his paws on the plane
like we practised. Now, he's holed up in the garden.

Holed up in the garden, the bear blooms like summer
from a creature to a god. I feed him from my hands

make myself small to sit in his shade. He's fascinated
by plants, how their leaves shake to help them grow

domesticating themselves. The bear cuts his teeth
on a silver key and lets himself inside, before cleaning

you away like bleach. His habits are getting harder
to predict. He holds parties every night and rabbits

every morning, juices snakes in the basement, high
on the extract. I sand the sharp edges of his ego.

Your own imperceptible stem surges in what's left
of the evening. The Guilt-Partridge is watching

speaking only in silence. I'm never naked anymore.
Sobriety is the only thing I've been promising myself.

I've been promising myself an hour at a time. Pausing
for each hand that swings for the twelve. I comb

through my arm. My bones are butter and pain.
The flowers you bought scream so loudly the room

is a church. Entirely unromantic, you called them.
The bear breathes it in; his lungs taste the petals

and grass. He takes black dregs of the toast outside
to the Guilt-Partridge. It gives me a scathing look

heavy, like swallowing a stone and feeling it sinking
along your breastbone. I wish I liked tea or coffee

so I could waste days making it. What else do I do
with so much time? If you want to be special, vanish

an inch at a time. I throw all the food in the house away
hoping to avert the crisis we were always heading for.

We were always heading for each other. Like the morning
a squirrel ran circles in the road before succumbing

to the tyres, flayed on the tarmac, undone, like a coat
lined with regret and muscle. In therapy, I can't stop

replaying her body, but I never confess. The bear tucks
a pencil behind his ear, looking over the rim of his glasses.

Judgement is drawn on a clipboard. Let the patient
speak first. I know it's a trick, so it doesn't work on me.

Remember, he smiles, *being turned on by your own skeleton?*
He was just the mirror. The doctor forms a warm frown

unable to see the whole room filling with a bear. I think
this is making me sicker. I leave, find my reflection

in the road, hoping it's not too late to save the squirrel.
Bargaining, the Guilt-Partridge sits on my shoulder.

The Guilt-Partridge sits on my shoulder in the service
station. Overpriced food and gambling are its only

commodities. In your buttons, you hold a post-mortem.
I look ashamed, like I'm meant to, slipping the batter off

onion rings like a day-old dress, the rubber strips
filling a plate. I take the fizz out of a diet coke, breathe

into its flatness. Paper disintegrates in the cup. I miss
plastic straws. The bear eats the potent white guts

until it makes him sick. The Guilt-Partridge whistles.
You should never be forgiven. I walk home because

it's good for me, pass the five-star hotel we lived in
for a month. Home is just where I keep emptying the bins.

The bear grabs my hand, his claw on my heartline.
My wrists itch. This is what inevitable feels like.

Inevitable feels like murmurs from the open chests
of the dead. *Nearly*, loops the Guilt-Partridge, writing

in the sky. One hour at a time. I think I'm okay. My best
friend's teaching English in Egypt so I can't call her.

The bear sends me messages and deletes the evidence.
I write help three times on my right leg. It spills over

the pavement. He ignores me, leaning against a lamppost
to lick honey from his claws, fished from a brown pot

as if to make a point about clichés and sharp objects.
The squirrel tends to her own crime scene, says hard

things through concrete teeth. The street is a war painting.
The bear hails a taxi and we all pile in. The Guilt-Partridge

takes the wheel. *Where to, love?* My insides are touching
everything. We won't be able to explain this at triage.

At triage, I tell half the truth. The bear gives me water
in a cup made of white atoms, and a conspiratorial look.

Everyone is sad, slumped in the backache of the wait.
The Guilt-Partridge taps at a screen. The pixels speak

of emergencies that will still take hours. They can't
prioritise the fallen. I lie my head on the lap of the bear.

His comfort feels dangerous, a barb suspended above
thought. *You make ordinary boys do such interesting things.*

On the ward, the bear sews me back together in single
nylon loops, until the grin is closed. There's a gulf

between us, between questions the professionals ask.
I make it home without being sectioned. The squirrel offers

her heart and some codeine. You still aren't impressed.
Petrol has gone up three pence in the last few hours.

In the last few hours I've gained forty new stitches.
Red is outliving me. I need to heal. It's not healthy

but it works. The bear lines up a paw with the wounds.
Look how far I was willing to go, what I left behind

how it's fixed but you can still see it. Grief is erotic
if you turn away for too long. The Guilt-Partridge sits

on the bear's lap, letting out bubbles that might mean
tears. The squirrel wraps herself in cling film to hide

the truth, to stop ideas pooling in her grazes. I layer
my own on tightly. Shower water drips down my body

like blood consommé. Six hundred days of recovery
drain down the sink. Undressing in front of animals

doesn't feel right. Liquid sears in every gap it fills.
Things have to change. This is a warning.

This is a warning, Bear. Leave. The council won't
allow the noise at this hour, and neither can I.

The air is toxic with cocktails; the liquor voices
of your wild guests ringing in the bone of china.

The inside-out Squirrel is dragging her guts along
the napkins, pushing the bread straight into her

digestive juices. These aren't the agreed principles
of proper food hygiene. Tea isn't served half milk.

Sugar can't be leftover stars. I dig through the bins
like a fox. Oh Bear, you should've cancelled the party.

Cracks in the cups keep letting the leaves out. It's far
too late, things are too delicate. Can't you see how

stained they are? Gorging on the relics of shame
the Guilt-Partridge hammers the crumbs left on the table.

RETCON

If you believe what you see on TV
dying is a reef knot, spilling
when you pull the end outward.

One day it's a stranger with a gun
the next it was the Sandman all along.
I kneel below your fist, stroking

my face, learn not to mind. I try
to write destructive things; you read
them out loud and they sound

so ordinary. Every time you retell
history, the future stays untouched.
I'll look for a different boy to be

successful with, pretend parts
of the timeline never existed.
The present is endless. The man

next door didn't just die some warm
weekday afternoon. He killed himself
before the tumour did. There must be

a reason why you're weak to yellow.
Pocket your guilt for a second —
it's the wrong way round, anyway.

The news has started forming
its own plot holes. The final problem
turns up alive in an empty house.

If I can endure sieges and sons
perhaps you could listen more.
It's not enough just to know —

there has to be some impact.
Resurrection becomes a dirty habit.
In Dallas, it's dream season again.

PAIN PERCEPTION OF CHICKEN EMBRYOS

There are neurons of a nervous system. There is a central brain.
I read the study on a late-night internet loop.
Pain can only be felt when this combination exists.

For the chicken embryo, this is the fifteenth day onwards.
Science disagrees about what happens before that.
I felt the first signs after three; nothing hurt instantly

blood takes a while to surface. As if it was saying
no way I'm sitting here waiting for you to need me
I'll get there when I get there.

THERE ARE NEURONS OF A NERVOUS SYSTEM

pain is a message	this isn't a symbol it's a truth	the aches medicines can't fix	every time yet think of the nurse
sewing my legs together	the stern patient she shouts at	they x-ray the wrong side of us	he walks on a fracture
something fragile an egg	shell break- ing even chickens	choose analgesics if needed	and I make it worse
living down my back bone	millipedes nothing else works	it's a problem I score	myself like a fish skin

ODORIGUI

it starts
in the dark room
wrong

a machine
standing upright
in the restaurant

its nerves a tower
salted flesh
from the bowl

they reach
out their dead
hands

to a small girl
drifting off
her bedroom floor

three times
a quiet voice
offers too much

to a beat up god
nothing happens
I think I'll sleep

with anyone
lips a blown
paperweight

a hallucination
of sodium intimacy
eyes me

with a hung fork
I break her
eight year old

clay pieces
throw them on the tiles
watching those

who don't get it
have a softer time
mourning he calls

her sad face
beautiful sinking
a squid creeps

under a trapdoor
saluting
the last line of life

BIRTH

They arrived in an incubator. We left the light on.
The kids watched the warm eggs cooked into life.

When the shells cracked, pecked through from hatching
the chicks began to exist. Motherless.

Two dead eggs sat between their siblings, a failure
of yolk. Their first breathing was caught on camera

e-mailed miles away, exhausted. Until it happened,
they were only ideas, calcium carbonate

then they broke alive. They were the last things
born before we swallowed the place whole.

LET THE WORLD END

I turn you off. I can't bear how you sound, the air
that hasn't passed into me for three weeks and two days.
In the rain I take eleven steps, watch the cloud whales

swim through the rooftops, breathe like a cold drum.
You used to feed me through a box, hindered
what I said. I can't listen to my voice distorted. I loved

everything about you. Lost keys, your looks, snakes
in the garden. Space in every song. I cradle a soaking
wet sparrow, draw lambs on fire. You have to imagine

how this sounds to people who've never seen the picture
in your notebook. I coat my lips with wax, from a bee
or maybe an orange. The truth is between a 2012 coffee shop

and being alone at a house party at the turn
of the millennium. I can't survive the thousand years
it'd take to change that, can't help you if I don't

exist. Not with furniture, money, wiping the dreams
from your face. We've stopped meaning the same things
walk through the city separately and if our paths

have crossed, you've left a mark in the litter. Parts
are cut away from the cathedral, a hole in my chest.
You drop the same excuses you did when you were young.

You still leave when you're finished. Talk about
what we lost and I hold up my hands cordiform. I thought
you meant me. I think I mean Laindon Station.

CAPACITY

T drives me to the coast for work, a black sky
feigns oblivion. I've been starving for months
done the stuff films tell you not to. There's less
of me to worry about. I once got so wet
nothing could help. Everything is closed;
off-season, empty like a spent hen.
I follow the road until it becomes a sea
straight-lining so I don't get lost. I'm not
sure how I'm getting through these nights.
The hamster is excavating its bed while I text
strangers. I can't sleep; he sweats in the alley
like a stray. She's a cheaper lover than I am
if she only writes you acrostic poems. T thinks
we'd make great travelling salesmen, glitters
when she tries it. I don't know how to be angry
except for those last two times. *I think we're going
to need another bottle.* I grieve old love on the glass
and the room like a mouth falls down.

BATTERY

girls are	eggs	key food	boys
kept for	technical	parts the	gassed
churning	ovoids	by-product	in boxes

preserved	macerated	sat through	constantly
in lifeless	macerated	a keynote	assault one
childhoods	and once	saying boys	another

for sex is	three young	are a few	fucking
a power	men in the	erections	macerating
move	seats opposite	away from	each other

so much	prey	empty eggs	relief or
progress yet	make good	pregnancy	a job
it's parent or	choices	tests	well done

CAMILLA

(The Muppets)

In the hen-yard, Gonzo chases purple girls but you keep
your eyes one colour. He can't understand it; you feel the same
each time. Every white feather feels like a white feather.

Bored, they want us to be different girls. I push a circle
of Levonelle through foil; he rubs the stitching of the steering
wheel. He asks me if I can believe the pharmacist thought

we were teenagers. No, I can't, because you're pushing forty
and I didn't even look sixteen when I was. We get it. Love
is a problem, a red scarf wrapped around your mouth.

When he was young, you were a ragdoll, only living
when he let you. I'm watching him read the instructions.
Perhaps he's a scientist. I'm the petri dish.

We go to bed on an empty floor. Forget you. I swallow hard
feel every sharp microgram. His whole body is blue and alien.
Even Wikipedia is in on the joke, on not really knowing what
   he is.

THE TIGER STAYED IN A TRAVELODGE

Nursing a heady Birmingham accent, the tiger smokes
discreetly. In a soundless bath he breathes brown:

a beery tan; teeth chewing a full pint glass. The tiger
stays in Travelodges. It's all his company can swing.

He'd never make mistakes with alarm system installation.
He smothers flames in a blanket, foam for organics, CO_2

for electricals. The tiger manages, professional to colleagues,
brought together for a week, a late job. They don't know

one other. The tiger married on New Year's Eve, calls his wife
a dog to strangers. It's now March. Better dog than tiger.

NATURE NURTURE

For the first few days, sex didn't matter
but of course it would. The clutch separated

gold from brown. Their colours were life or death
decisions, but aren't they all? We're always who

we are — the problem comes when we notice.
You can't keep boys, you see. Too noisy

plus they compromise the girls. A man collected
them, said things about humanity and euthanasia.

It was best not to ask questions. The girls were left
to grow, they did this quickly — good farm birds.

They never saw a completed chicken, yet
they perched around the rim of their box

on the same Sunday, kicked up the woodchips
foraged, flapped. They just knew what to do.

ANY CONSOLATION

haven't you seen tracks and doubled back before?
the hole where you buried sounds by the leopard

print of your skin, alive with air tonight you push
your fingertips into my eyes when you want to know

how wet things are; how warm the sockets feel
I said I love you to the dead dial tone, did everything

I could except bring a bag of moles. I underestimate
the guilt that you have for everyone else despite

the list of symptoms, I have all of them but anger.
it's like looking at red for so long that the world

is green when you stop. didn't we discuss
my diagnosis on the plane?

how base you can be, I kept all your unreads
I know I should've split at that altitude.

PREDATOR THEORY

waiting to be lucky	coyotes get city desperate	hunting grounds shrinking	raccoons pick locks
beautiful girls wear spiders	prey animals only	touched for sex or food	I take a man who isn't you
to bed wish I could call you	names as foxes haunt the rabbits	there's no blood just nudes	miles from the murder
you think you're subtle	it doesn't happen like this	in the rainforests but there	are none in Great Yarmouth

THE TIGER MAKES PROMISES

Drunk on the cuts of broken girls, the tiger escorts
them to their bedrooms, so he knows where they go

when they're vulnerable; the doors they are stored
behind to sleep. He smiles in a low growl, never

self-compromises. The tiger breathes unfathomable
hunger into the mouths of the ones who find it

better to eat than burn. He promises your best friend
that he'll get you home. He keeps his word. Wounds

can't help but cross paths when alcohol blurs them.
He can leave you anywhere. He knows the way back.

BEAR COUNTRY

At a cookout in the mountains, we're talking about bears
while firelight is reaching through the dark for our faces.

The evening lasts for miles. I used to see maps and think
London was made of stations surrounded by empty space.

Canada is really like that. The creaking owner of the ranch
is talking about two things I've only seen in North America:

guns and smores. He is made of silver lines and serious looks
covered in the country. Heat melts the marshmallows, licking

their corners black. He takes a bite. The intention goes off
silently. Things are always softer in the middle. My mother

says you never see stars where we are, but I'm sure I have.
If it's dark enough you can see Ursa Major from anywhere

in the northern hemisphere. My thoughts are at least three
conversations ago. *If one came up here, I'd have to shoot.*

All I can think of is how long a barrel must be to end a bear.
Doubt is such a giveaway. *Yes*, he says. Without hesitation.

IT'S TOO LATE FOR VISITORS

I hold the night to my ear, it echoes
like a seashell. I've made an enemy
of quiet. The walls are moving. Light
is chanting loudly in the bathroom.
I press my face onto cold tiles, dream
of being arterial all over the floor.
My hips have suffered enough;
I've exploded all their architecture.
The door coughs a knock, a virus
in the dark. It's too late for visitors
to not have drunk terrible wine
by the bottle. Five chicks hatched
at the school today. If I can get home
something might finally need me.

REASONABLE BELIEF

The sky is falling. I catch silence hiding
in the wrong house, only breathe in

specific corners. A body sits on my back.
It's funny, what it makes you think about.

I can't remember if my last time was you
or some prick at Heathrow Airport

but it's been more than six months
a year since you taught me there are ways

to say yes or no. Every book I read
is trying to start a war and the meat I buy

lies about where it came from — the signs
saying so are made of paper. Two swans

slice through mud, thick as the night
as cold eating out annihilation. Spit

washes you away for good, his fingers
rest on things you don't know I did

for you. My feelings are a chest freezer.
I don't want to taste of ice and rosé

here, without my hands. The first time
you got her pregnant it took you three years

to speak to me again. Now you're just
fucking where you can fit it in. My mouth

is blue. I suck wet air through the sheets.
The sky is falling. This was just the first crumb.

LATE ROOST

It's my turn to put the girls away and I've forgotten.
The TV laughs. We've spent all these weekends together
I've killed too many things already. Therapy isn't helping.

Jamie Oliver is electrocuting one live with Paul
a professional slaughterer. *It's never nice* he says,
but you get used to it. I worry about the efficacy of chickens

what too late truly means. Take corners quickly
on the drive, break in through the gates telling myself
faster, don't be the thing that gets the girls hurt.

They need to be high up to feel safe at night. Gordon
could do this with his eyes shut. He puts on a blindfold
the crowd brays. He feels out a joint and puts a knife

right through it. I wonder if it's precision or method
that affects how we taste. The enclosure is empty;
coop centred like a castle in a dead courtyard.

It's only dusk; the security light doesn't need to try
so hard. They've taken themselves inside already. Good girls.
Shutting the door, I breathe the night relief. All is well.

HANGOVER

I'm still swimming. Only four hours passed
since I went to bed, still a little bloody. I spat
my teeth out in the bath, sieved him well out of it.

The room spins. I dress forgettable. I used to wear
heels even for work. Not anymore. I send T a text
to say that I'm ready, but my veins are still full.

The corridor seems shorter, less infinite in light.
T greets me with a smile. She had enough rosé herself
to know how much there is in my head. The grease

of breakfast isn't punishment enough. There's only
one place left to eat. I'm not sure how to feel.
I watch the door, check who comes in. No-one does.

T's less excited by the hotel's conveyor belt toaster.
Did you hear him say he would? she says, flattered.
I say I did. The details are irrelevant.

The cuts in my leg are burning. I wonder why he asked
about them, and then did it anyway. Did what exactly?
I don't know yet. It took a few days — remember?

STEPS TAKEN

It's impossible to know all the insects.
You should be able to name things
that crawl over your heels, look
them up; feel sick over facts and family
photos. You pull strands of brain out
twist them into a wasp's nest. *No* means
lick me like a picnic table. Summer brims
with poisonous caterpillars, spines
painted like piano teeth. The field
is digging in, its creases stinging
like blue laces. A skin beetle inches up
my arm. If we were starlings, we might steal
ants straight from each other's mouths.
I didn't say you could touch me. Earwigs
cluster in the footwell, trying to understand.

LADY KLUCK

(Robin Hood, 1973)

Here's a weird question, what's the instrument the rooster plays
in the animal version of *Robin Hood*? In the play we did at school
I couldn't work out how his name was a pun, because it wasn't.

All my favourite men write music. I'm sharing a sofa with one
who's telling me he was once asked if it was the chicken
who influenced his taste in bigger women. I don't know which

of the things he says are the ones he means; he's sure
the moon is full every night. I see it disappearing.
There are too many calories in humiliation.

I've already tried being smaller than the boys who left me.
I loved starving. Everyone else did too; I ate nothing
but their praise. All three times he gave it were accidental.

I lick the fork clean. It's like eating all day breakfast from a can.
It's the meat that makes it gruesome, truthful, like every inch
of a room with the light on. He's the rehearsal. I'm getting off

on watching him slip away his belt, like the muscle
of a snake wrapped around his hand. I flinch at the buckle.
It's bringing out the blood in me. *A lute*, I say.

BLOOD IS THICKER

I'm running away and the river helps. Greenery blurs.
Focussing on each leaf is migraine territory. I'm boxing

up my own plans in favour of my brother's, conducting
suicide watch by text. How our parents made us share

our worst parts, when we haven't done the same things
not stayed in the same hotels, not been black-eyed

by the same boys — just sat together on the backseat
of an argument, complained about the babysitter, caught

a french mouse in a saucepan. You have to be careful
who you mix with. What the plans are. How the other

side of the bed holds a dog. I want to live closer to sky
than a ceiling will let me. On the stairs this morning

I faced our father, wrapped like wet meat in a towel
knowing all there is to know and all he can say is he doesn't

remember where the carpet went, that he wants acrylic paint
for Christmas. Wasn't your favourite colour always red?

INDUSTRY

robots x- ray eggs candling	their lives out machines	trundle by newborns	fill boxes like cities hands winch
away the weak-eyed palmed	like close-up magic I stay	empty ideas aren't enough	hospital tubes laced up
in after- thought still	bubble with blood	I create words not flesh	watch your lust fizz away
like a slug on copper	life is cut out of all of us	a handful of YouTube comments	still calling this humane

REMAINS

My friends formed a line of bad news that morning. *We're sorry*

they said. *We have something to tell you.* There's no delicate way

to say it. Years ago I read a piece about sailboats at a wake

thought I'd be fine because I barely knew her. No-one warned me

the air can be so sad you can't breathe it in anymore. *They kill*

more than they can eat; the rest gets left behind. The man from

the RSPCA talked for so long about wounds. I was already

an expert. He was certain it was foxes. Agreed it was a lot of blood.

I'm ringing post-sex, and it's bright and traumatic. He's in Yarmouth

he knows how I feel about that. I spelled involve wrong, now it has love

in it, which is a regretful word for an e-mail. The chicks sob into the soil

from their bin sack, so black my eyes stick together. It's nice to see

the winter ducks return. I should report this to Defra.

Not everything gets a funeral. There's not always enough left.

RITUALS

I step on the scale, it replies with bad news.
There's usually a dog here but today he's out

undergoing a heart bypass. No-one could hold
him still enough. I count everything — grains

of rice, time spent awake, holes in skulls, how
deep they go. Sea birds swim the second

they hit the water. I'm looking for numbers
not nourishment. The television keeps turning

itself off. A letter of complaint falls through
the door stagnating on the carpet. There are no

pain receptors in the brain but I'm still
getting headaches. I cut myself wide open.

The fence must wonder why it's getting
the blame for what I did when I was drunk.

You burn half of what you eat just by staying
alive. I don't know how to be hungry.

I'll have to do more to provoke it —
stop mixing shots and instinct together.

MIKE

You're impossible. The remains of an axe clot
like a plug in the sink. Keep the only ear you've got
to the ground and hope it finishes you off. It's taken

nearly everything - your eyes, your tongue, a decent
but not fatal percentage of your brain. They'll call you
a miracle but you feel like a freak so you run, swearing

you once had a face and what a face, as it lies
on the board below. They clear your throat for you
you need help with that now your neck is a cave.

You sleep in different beds. You're just a body
you apologise for. Keep trying. It's just nerves.
It means nothing. Other men line up for their chance

a cut in the right direction leaving just enough of you
behind. If you stopped, the feel of light on your brainstem
would be excruciating and they'd cheer anyway.

There's more to living than putting the right things in:
grain, air, other people. You suffocate months after dying.
Birds, unlike us, balance themselves lower down.

IKIZUKURI

I turn up too bright for care or conversation
see through my wilting skin. I need more

signs that we're living: snoring into pillows
running out of sleep. a therapist once

gave me a book, told me not to use it
as an instruction manual, but some things

are so easy to imagine, you have to check
them for yourself. I'm serving myself up

in a seafood restaurant still breathing
as they pick my stomach away in slices

sad in your disappointment, your softness
when you want me, carving out stripes

of lionfish. love is for the soundless
the science of animals. how is it, dying

in such careful sections? you have to know
there are few advantages to living this way.

I see why you want to stop. in the notes
she's writing the last few letters down.

FAULTS

Trauma busies red cells; healing is a compromise.
You're like plasma: the sense of you, promising
but tasteless. People can feel either way about scars.

I pulled my own heart out from here
so it had to be incredible, drank away
the nerves before five freckles fell in.

Cut out the bits that have gone bad —
it's my mother's approach to preservation.
If the bread has gone stale it makes better toast.

On her shoulder there's a bite mark, the fist
of an island where the skin seized up. Kneeling
beside me, you throw the wine bottle down.

My brother split his head on a coffee table
like this I learned about butterfly stitches
only to spend years looking into wounds

to see what I was made of. I came down
with the flu in a lecture theatre. Drank
the warm blood of pigs at a leaving party.

I'm having regular fantasies about trepanning.
You ask for the cane and it sings one clear note
slicing open the air. I'm sleeping with more

than one man who has psoriasis. Magic is spilling
out of my head. We're both so vulnerable
neither of us knows who's bleeding.

BILLINA

(Return to Oz)

Where is your egg, Billina? asks Dorothy. She hasn't slept
in months. Her aunt is concerned by the stories she tells —
needs of lions, an upside-down house.

The only flood is on the screen. I'm twelve days
late. Patience is the only thing I'm leaking. My spine
crunches into snails; filling a cup with myself.

The morning makes me stronger. He is moving
house, arguing with his ex-wife. Dorothy is holding
her contraband hen. I'm waiting for a cross to appear

in my urine. I'm waiting for a faint blue stab.
Where is your egg? It's such a soft night to sleep in.
I'm not trying to start a fight — it's his fault.

I keep coming out clean. If you don't want to be found
hide in the heads of others. An oval plummets into the mouth
of the concrete king. There are two bank holidays this week

I need to see a doctor now. The line is still a line.
I look up what became of Billina. She stayed in Oz
had dozens of chicks. No one mentions the father.

THE TIGER EVOLVES IMMUNITY

The tiger evolves immunity, but not anonymity.
It takes a few basic search terms to find him.

He smiles in group photographs, arms around
the lads, salutes the sky with an 8 iron. Each time

you check there's more. A knife in a wedding
cake. He'll have a child. This is how it works.

She'll be round, rosy, and when he holds her
no-one will worry enough about what he's done

what he'll do, who else knows, if he prowls
over her at night in case others come out.

NIGHTLINES

This is terminal. I'm a poor decision
maker. All these men are grey
and it makes me want one more.
The length of the night is white
with pavement through the moon.
If you say enough to strangers
something has to stick. Share
indiscretions, seats, frustrations.
Share too much in weeknight bars
faithless bite on the glass, pile out
onto the wet streets whispering
you can tell me anything, I promise.
I'll die in love before judgement.
Under the bent neck of a lamppost
shake hands with a fat tongue soaked
in whiskey, notice the tilted curiosity
of pigeons. I'm never scared of being
alone in the dark, not now I've only
been split in warm places. I'm not
in any position to call you back.

RECOVERY LOOKS DIFFERENT ON EVERYONE

I take my sadness to the bathtub, wipe the walls clean. red feathers grow from my ankles. I practise drowning three times a week, it burns like the chlorine in San Francisco. I summon a slow mouth of spit for a painkiller. *Mark* says I've become more beautiful since he's known me, but he really means smaller — I've got to get over him. I used to tie a ribbon around my thigh, then cut it in leaving breaks so the whole thing wouldn't collapse. I don't think there's a sin I haven't committed in this building. I check them off. *Nick* says this is no surprise, you seek what hurt you to heal, but Nick speaks about being a pro golfer like it's an act of terrorism and lives with a sixty-year-old woman who he's trying to persuade to piss into his hands. he swears she's considering it. I wonder how many guests have been in this kitchen. the dark blue is gorgeous and I could suck you to death on the stools that open like oysters. *Paul* makes insightful points, like people who are good at sex aren't good at relationships. I've already had one bad review today. my heart needs things now.

it's 2016 again, and my legs are a swamp. I wear black and a long necklace. the fireplace is a looped video on a flatscreen and I only want what I'm not doing. *Nigel* talks about raincoats and how single he is, but he doesn't know I've found his wife on a dating app. fear is a small room, and my friends tell me I'm scared of so much it's become meaningless. *New Mark* says heights aren't the problem, it's the worry you might throw yourself off, but he works in a bank and likes fisting. the balcony drops me into the open night. *Kevin* says sweet things, but he only has to say them down the phone, and that makes it easier. *Tom* says nothing, but he says it in French. it's always the morning after, when my eyes are like a zebra's. I move the cutlery away from my imagination. *Simon* asks, what was the best year of your life? I'm still thinking about the answer. I text four people the same thing. hoarding is a disorder of anxiety. *Ben* says I'm all talk. I hold the blade between my teeth. I am all truth.

SALT & EGGS

Dipping a finger into an egg
just to find the centre lacks salt
like lying on concrete in daytime
dream-sick, rising through the soul
until it all gives out
in confessions over breakfast.

The morning after, breakfast
felt no different. I ate eggs
the same way, carving yolks out
their chambers, white like salt
nerveless souls
still the same. Every time

since the first one is like this. Taking time
to pretend that breakfast
is enough to cleanse the soul.
I hit myself in the stomach; where eggs
swim without morals or reason or salt
water, and I can't drink enough to get them out.

I might need to check out
more than vomit this time.
I look up the side effects of salt
and remember a boy, once at breakfast
tipping a packet onto the yolk of an egg
eating it whole, so effervescent that its soul

was gone. Truth sticks in the soul
when it's too much, like finding out
that birds come from eggs
then hoping they don't come alive over time
in a horror story over breakfast.

Swallow. Pass the salt.

I use the wrong word — I only say assault.
Like it wasn't me, but some poor soul
feeling lost over breakfast
while the pan sweats out
one yellow eye at a time
the blooming parachute of an egg.

Again and again, at breakfast, salt whites the film
leaving stains on the egg. Its bright soul
dries out in streaks; life leaving it, all this time.

PTEROTILLOMANIA

there are parts of you
that don't belong
you pull them out
you see it
these birds, bald
racing to rip their own colours
from their chests, their humans
dress them in tiny jumpers
who doesn't love
an animal in clothes
stroke your whole body
one at a time
these strands of self
are dangerous
pretend you're not
the reason a bright bird
turns herself pink
captives fall apart
well, they don't fall
they orchestrate
their own amputations
tear a self
from skin, press
what comes in thousands
between the fat of the lips
too many times
everything loses its joy

WITHOUT SLEEPING

the sky is a ceiling of rain and the bed lasts
from here to the north. you aren't sorry

for either. you describe what it's like to live
normally in your oxford voice and i tell you

stories that blow the world out. before 4am
you were there, cerebral, car stolen, gutted

glass shell. you sleep noiselessly through it.
it will be harder to finish if one of us dies

so i look for changes, the number of hands
the length of empty linen, the tone you cry in —

take words away and everyone's an animal.
i'm sorry alex, this is the best i can do. it's easy

like this; it's reality that cracks things up. when
night touches me it feels like my flesh is paint

peeling off and how can you understand
that i'm about as buoyant as i'm going to get —

LEAVE OF ABSENCE

If anyone knew what I was listening to, they'd be ashamed.
I'd say, it's not the song, it's this exact moment, but it wouldn't
make it forgivable. The day is consuming in unhealthy doses.
A man takes a drink and I realise it's been a week already.
Rebecca can't come to work today, her life is too boring. A van
has fallen into this side of the motorway and no-one calls you
back when they say they will. The roads are full of death
and the inevitable potential for it. There's a cat smashed
into a curl, then all anyone talks about all day is cats. When
there are humans around to miss things, tragedy is acceptable.
Rebecca can't come to work today she's researching cat funeral songs.
I pass this nature reserve every day, an overgrown scrub
no one has money to maintain, which proves it's how you name
things not what they are. A man takes a drink and his car growls
to increase the pressure. *Rebecca can't come to work today
there's too much of the earth to tend to.* Six squirrels fell in
an uncovered water trough. The boy who found them loved
violence until he made it real. He's only eight. I cut out shapes
of grief; all hexagons. A man takes a drink in a bar and half
the girls in there are sabotaged. *Rebecca can't come to work today.
She's covered in imaginary spiders.* I'll never sustain what I give
myself: cocktails, this step count, stability. I throw away
warm water ; I didn't pay for it, so no sunk costs. *Rebecca can't
come to work today.* Diazepam is not a party drug. I call a boy
who only identifies with half of himself in public. No answer.
A man takes a drink and I figure things are bad enough.
I've had them in the wrong order, like matryoshka dolls
that don't fit inside each other. My heart is a nature reserve.
It's a shame that the face of someone who knows
what they're doing has to be this one.

ACKNOWLEDGEMENTS

Thank you and all my love to my family for your support, understanding and humour.

Thank you to Claire for being there all these years, often in fancy hotels, struggling to make decisions. Thank you to Ashleigh and Jason – friends and colleagues – for all the collective effervescence. Thank you to Terri, Vicky, Richard, Kelly and Carly, for friendship, adventure, residentials and Thursdays. Thank you to Jack for encouragement and music.

Thank you to Anthony Anaxagorou, for all your wisdom, sense of humour and belief in my work. I have really appreciated and enjoyed working with you.

Thank you to Patricia Ferguson for all your help and skill in making these words a book.

Thank you to my fellow poets for inspiring me with your own work, your friendship and feedback, and listening to an awful lot of things about chickens, particularly Alex Collins, Anita Kafka, Shibani Kaushik, Ana Patricia Medina Castillo, Louise Vaughan, Navkiran Kaur Mann, Charlotte Stokes Meyer Zu Natrup, Adam Cairns and Tim Relf.

Thank you to all of my teachers – particularly Rachael Allen, Daljit Nagra and Pele Cox.

Thank you to Clare French for the title, the commitment to coming up with one, and for sharing stories of your own chicken.

Thank you to *Propel*, *The Poetry Review* and *berlin lit* who first published some of these poems.

Rebecca McCutcheon is a poet and educator living on the Essex coast. Her work has appeared in *The Poetry Review*, *Propel Magazine* and *berlin lit*.

SELECTED OTHER TITLES BY OUT-SPOKEN PRESS

Bark, Archive Splinter • JAY GAO
Boiled Owls • AZAD ASHIM SHARMA
[...] • FADY JOUDAH
Vulgar Errors / Feral Subjects • FRAN LOCK
State of Play: Poets of East & Southeast Asian Heritage in Conversation • EDS. EDDIE TAY & JENNIFER WONG
Nude as Retrospect • ALEX MARLOW
Today Hamlet • NATALIE SHAPERO
G&T • OAKLEY FLANAGAN
sad thing angry • EMMA JEREMY
Trust Fall • WILLIAM GEE
Cane, Corn & Gully • SAFIYA KAMARIA KINSHASA
apricot • KATIE O'PRAY
Mother of Flip-Flops • MUKAHANG LIMBU
Dog Woman • HELEN QUAH
Caviar • SARAH FLETCHER
Somewhere Something is Burning • ALICE FRECKNALL
flinch & air • LAURA JANE LEE
Fetch Your Mother's Heart • LISA LUXX
Seder • ADAM KAMMERLING
54 Questions for the Man Who Sold a Shotgun to My Father • JOE CARRICK-VARTY
Lasagne • WAYNE HOLLOWAY-SMITH
Mutton Rolls • ARJI MANUELPILLAI
Contains Mild Peril • FRAN LOCK
Epiphaneia • RICHARD GEORGES
Stage Invasion: Poetry & the Spoken Word Renaissance • PETE BEARDER
The Neighbourhood • HANNAH LOWE
The Games • HARRY JOSEPHINE GILES
Songs My Enemy Taught Me • JOELLE TAYLOR
To Sweeten Bitter • RAYMOND ANTROBUS